TERRIFIC TEAMS

Meet the NEW YORK YANKEES

ZELDA WAGNER

Lerner Publications ◆ Minneapolis

Stats in this book are accurate through the 2024 Major League Baseball season.

Lerner Publications Company
An imprint of Lerner Publishing Group, Inc.
241 First Avenue North
Minneapolis, MN 55401 USA

For reading levels and more information, look up this title at www.lernerbooks.com.

Main body text set in ITC Avant Garde Gothic Std.
Typeface provided by Adobe Systems.

Editor: Elena Mai
Lerner team: Sue Marquis

Library of Congress Cataloging-in-Publication Data

Names: Wagner, Zelda, 2000- author
Title: Meet the New York Yankees / Zelda Wagner.
Description: Minneapolis, MN : Lerner Publications, [2026] | Series: Terrific teams (Lerner sports rookie) | Includes bibliographical references and index. | Audience: Ages 5–8 | Audience: Grades 2–3 | Summary: "The New York Yankees have won 27 World Series titles. They hold the record for the most World Series wins by any MLB team. Discover more about the team's history, best players, and greatest moments"— Provided by publisher.
Identifiers: LCCN 2025015093 (print) | LCCN 2025015094 (ebook) | ISBN 9798765689684 library binding | ISBN 9798348029449 paperback | ISBN 9798765699386 epub
Subjects: LCSH: New York Yankees (Baseball team)—History—Juvenile literature | Baseball players—United States—Juvenile literature | Baseball—New York (State)—New York—History—Juvenile literature
Classification: LCC GV875.N4 W34 2026 (print) | LCC GV875.N4 (ebook) | DDC 796.357/64097471—dc23/eng/20250509

LC record available at https://lccn.loc.gov/2025015093
LC ebook record available at https://lccn.loc.gov/2025015094

Manufactured in the United States of America
1-1012409-54836-7/8/2025

Photo Acknowledgments
Image credits: AP Photo/Godofredo Vásquez, p. 5; AP Photo/Sue Ogrocki, p. 7; Bettmann/Getty Images, pp. 9, 13; Jed Jacobsohn/Getty Images, p. 11; AP Photo/Nick Wass, p. 14; AP Photo/Seth Wenig, p. 16; New York Yankees/Getty Images, p. 18; Jim McIsaac/Getty Images, p. 20; AP Photo/Tom E. Puskar, p. 22; AP Photo/Gregory Fisher/Icon Sportswire, p. 23. Design elements: Kwangmoozaa/Getty Images; Andrii Shelenkov/Getty Images; jasonclardy/Getty Images.
Cover: AP Photo/Ashley Landis.

Table of Contents

In October 2024, Aaron Judge batted for the New York Yankees. Home run!

Judge's home run helped the Yankees win Game 2 of the ALCS.

Four days later, the Yankees won the ALCS. They were AL champs!

The Yankees have won the AL 41 times. They hold the record for the most AL wins.

Big Moments

The Yankees history is full of great plays. In 1921, the Yankees won the AL for the first time.

Two years later, the Yankees won their first World Series. They beat the New York Giants in six games.

Between 1923 and 2000, the Yankees won 26 World Series.

In 2009, the Yankees won their 27th World Series. That is the most World Series wins of any MLB team.

Best Players

In 1920, Babe Ruth joined the New York Yankees. Ruth was the best home run hitter in MLB.

Ruth helped the Yankees win four World Series.

Derek Jeter played with the Yankees for 20 seasons. He is sixth in MLB history with 3,465 hits.

In 2022, Aaron Judge hit 62 home runs. He set an AL record for most home runs in a season.

Judge is also the fastest player to reach 300 career home runs.

Since 1957, the Gold Glove Award has been given to the best fielders in MLB.

In 2023, Anthony Volpe became the first Yankees rookie to win the Gold Glove Award.

Since 1923, the Yankees have played at Yankee Stadium in the Bronx, New York.

A new Yankee Stadium opened in 2009. It has a special place to honor past superstars.

The Yankees have fans all over the world.

With Aaron Judge and Anthony Volpe leading the way, the Yankees will keep breaking records.

NEW YORK YANKEES TEAM LEADERS

Batting average:	Babe Ruth, .349
Hits:	Derek Jeter, 3,465
Home runs:	Babe Ruth, 659
Wins:	Whitey Ford, 236
Strikeouts:	Andy Pettitte, 2,020

Glossary

AL: American League

ALCS: American League Championship Series

MLB: Major League Baseball

rookie: a player in their first season

Learn More

Leed, Percy. *Baseball: A First Look*. Lerner Publications, 2023.

Leed, Percy. *Baseball Superstars*. Lerner Publications, 2025.

Leed, Percy. *Baseball's World Series*. Lerner Publications, 2025.

Index